Finish Line Thinking™
How to Think and Win Like a Champion
2nd Edition

by
Nicky Billou

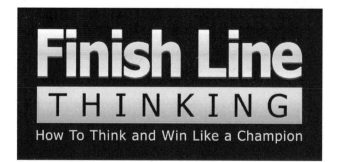

Finish Line Thinking™
How to Think and Win Like a Champion
Copyright 2014 Nicky Billou

13 digit ISBN 978-1500713553
10 digit ISBN 1500713554

Table of Contents

Foreword to the 2nd Edition 4

Introduction 5

What is the Finish Line Thinking Program™? 6

The Dictionary Definition of Champion..7

The 13 Principles of Thinking and Winning like a Champion: 8

1. Embrace Healthy Eating as a Lifestyle 8

2. Embrace Daily Exercise...9

3. Expect to Win...10

4. Actively surround yourself with the support you need to win 12

5. Become part of a community of supportive like-minded peers.........13

6. Set BIG goals 15

7. Embrace failure, and fail fast...16

8. Get the best coach, not just a great coach 18

9. Develop the Heart of a Champion...20

10. You're either addicted or committed. Commit...............................22

11. Seek to be held accountable by your Community of Champions.....24

12. Embrace Mastery...26

13. Take on Daily Disciplines..28

    1. Daily Exercise & Healthy Eating...29

    2. Daily Success Rituals 29

    3. Daily De-stressing 33

    4. Daily Accountability 33

    5. Daily Commitments..33

Bonus! 6. Daily Finish Line Thinking™ 28

The Finish Line Thinking Scorecard™...35

Get Help With Winning at Your Finish Line 41

Hire Nicky Billou to Speak at Your Next Event.....................................42

Foreword to the 2nd Edition

I am an athletic Champion, winner of 15 National Championships, 3 Commonwealth Games Championships, an Olympic Gold Medal, and 3 world records. I know a thing or two about how champions think, and I can tell you unequivocally that is the most important factor in making them a champion.

I have beaten people with equal talent, simply because my mindset was stronger than theirs, and I have seen countless talented individuals lose in sport and business because they didn't have the mindset of a champion. Conversely, I have seen people with few natural gifts embrace the mindset of a champion, and use that mindset to develop the skills they needed to win in business and in life, and I have seen them win spectacularly.

I have known Nicky for over 10 years, and he is someone who has made it his business to study champions and what makes them tick. He is very curious, and during the time I have known him, he has peppered me with literally hundreds of questions about how I think and how it's helped me achieve what I have achieved. He himself is a champion speaker, one of the best I have ever seen.

He has also coached and mentored numerous champions in sport and business, and studied how they do what they do, and he has helped teach them how to think and win like a champion. He gets it, he lives it, and more importantly, he is passionate about helping you get it and live it, too.

The principles he has outlined in this book work, and the success stories he has shared here powerfully illustrate them in action. I highly recommend you read this book, watch his videos on YouTube, and put them into action for yourself. You'll be glad you did.

Mark McKoy
1992 Olympic Gold Medalist, 110 m hurdles
3-time world record holder

Introduction

Back in 2003, a good friend of mine introduced me to a genuine Canadian sports hero, Olympic Gold Medalist Mark McKoy, winner of the 110 m Olympic Gold Medal at the 1992 Barcelona Olympics. Mark in turn introduced me to another Olympic Gold Medalist. The 3 of us got into business together, and Mark and I became friends.

Soon after, I became fascinated by these 2 champions, and how different their thinking was than the rest of us. They seemed to be thinking and operating at a completely different level than anyone else I had ever met. I began to research the whole subject of how your thinking -- attitudes, beliefs, mindset – influenced your ability to produce results. I began working with thought leaders like Robin Sharma and Raymond Aaron, athletes like ultra-distance runner and Guinness World Record Holder Theresa Dugwell, and business titans like Bruce Poon Tip and Gil Blutrich (champions all in their respective fields) and painstakingly began piecing together a philosophy and a program for how champions think.

Why?

Because how a champion thinks is **THE** decisive factor in what makes him a champion. His thoughts, his attitudes, his beliefs are so precise that they allow him to win. It's what allowed an ordinary woman like Theresa Dugwell to establish and break ultra-distance Guinness World Records, it's what allowed an unknown like Robin Sharma to be one of the world's top business and spiritual gurus, it's what allowed a skinny kid named Mark McKoy to become Canada's first Track & Field Olympic Gold Medalist in 60 years.

And it's what will allow **_YOU_** to become a champion in your own right, in your chosen area of endeavor, if you take the time to learn and apply these principles.

What is the Finish Line Thinking Program™?

Finish Line Thinking™ is a unique and exclusive program designed to teach you the ambitious, happy, fun, positive and successful business professional how to think and win like a champion. Being a champion is not just for athletes. It is for people involved in all kinds of endeavors — business, academics, spelling bees, etc. You can be any kind of champion, not just an athletic champion. This program teaches you the 13 Principles of Thinking and Winning like a Champion. These Principles are:

1. Embrace Healthy Eating as a Lifestyle
2. Embrace Daily Exercise as a Lifestyle
3. Expect to win
4. Actively surround yourself with the support you need to win
5. Become part of a community of supportive like-minded peers
6. Set BIG goals
7. Embrace failure, and fail fast
8. Get the best coach, not just a great coach
9. Have the heart of a champion
10. You're either addicted or committed. Commit
11. Seek to be held accountable
12. Embrace Mastery
13. Take on Daily Disciplines

The most important principle is #13: Take on Daily Disciplines. Ask any champion and he will tell you, what makes him a champion is that he has a series of daily disciplines that he follows religiously. To double your current success rate, and cross that Finish Line as a champion, you need to take on daily disciplines that you stick to, just like a champion. Daily Disciplines Are What Champions Do!

The 5 Most Important Daily Disciplines:
1. Daily Exercise & Healthy Eating
2. Daily Success Rituals
3. Daily De-stressing
4. Daily Accountability
5. Daily Commitments

Bonus!

6. Daily Finish Line Thinking™

The Dictionary Definition of Champion

cham·pi·on - *n.*

1. One that wins first place or first prize in a competition:
2. One that is clearly superior or has the attributes of a winner:
3. An ardent defender or supporter of a cause or another person:
4. One who fights; a warrior. adj.
5. Holding first place or prize:

The 13 Principles of Thinking and Winning like a Champion:

1. Embrace Healthy Eating as a Lifestyle

Champions get it. They know that having optimal health and energy is critical to being a champion. They don't argue with themselves about this. They know they have to work out and eat right. They embrace it as a lifestyle. To be a champion yourself, you must do the same. Let me ask you a question. How many overweight, out of shape, diabetic athletic champions do you know? None? Me neither.

Whether your goal is to be the top CEO in your industry, or the top salesman in your office, or the first woman to be the richest person in your country, you've got to take care of your health. One, optimal health will help you get there, and two, don't you want to be healthy enough to enjoy your success?

Embrace Healthy Eating. All champions do.

Ask yourself this question: How can I improve my eating habits so that they are optimizing my health?

Success story:

Ben Katebian is the CEO of Moneygate Corporation, a Financial Services firm. Ben took on changing his eating habits, lost 15 pounds and increased his energy massively! This has allowed him to deal with the ongoing challenges of a growing business far more effectively and efficiently.

"Finish Line Thinking™ and Nicky's coaching have made a massive difference in helping me focus on optimizing my health. I lost 15 pounds in less than 3 months, I now have lots more energy, and my productivity and performance have increased significantly as a result. Taking on Embracing Daily Healthy Eating has made all the difference!"

2.   Embrace Daily Exercise

Champions workout every day. They know that to optimize their health, they have to move their bodies to keep them in top shape. That is impossible without daily exercise. Which means every day, not every day except weekends and holidays, or days when your schedule is insanely busy.

Daily exercise doesn't necessarily mean going to the gym 2 hours a day. If you can do that, great, go for it. But if your schedule really is packed and carving out two hours isn't an option, commit to at least 10 minutes a day, no matter what. Set your timer to 10 minutes on your smart phone and go for a walk or a jog, or contact me by email (*info@ finishlinethinking.com*) and I'll send you a workout e-book for a home based workout you can do that's 20 minutes long. (I know, it's not 10 minutes, but you can start by just doing 10 minutes of it.)

Ask yourself this question: How can I embrace daily exercise?

Success story:

Louie Santaguida is the founder and CEO of Stanton Renaissance, a builder and developer of major condominium projects in Southern Ontario. A former athlete in his teens and early twenties, by his early forties he had given up his formerly good habits of daily exercise.

Today, Louie has embraced daily exercise to the point that he now participates in a series of grueling annual desert races, where he runs across deserts like the Sahara, the Gobi, and Antarctica every year. To prepare for these races, he has to exercise every day, and the benefit to him has been that his energy has increased, and this has helped him elevate his performance in a fast-moving industry.

"Since I began working with Nicky and his system, I have been exercising daily, and my energy has skyrocketed. I run a fast-paced multimillion dollar business, and having peak energy is critical for me to keep on top of everything. Finish Line Thinking™ really works!"

3. Expect to Win

Champions expect to win.

Michael Johnson, the great 200m and 400m Olympic Champion, a 4-time Olympic Gold Medalist and 8-time World Champion, once wore specially made gold shoes by Nike. These shoes were paper-thin and super-light, designed for single-use only. They cost a lot of money, and Michael would throw them into the crowd after each race.

A reporter once asked him, "Michael, how come you are wearing gold shoes? What if you lose? Won't you be embarrassed?"

Michael replied "I run to win. I don't think about losing, I think about winning."

That says it all.

My mentor Olympic Champion Mark McKoy once told me that whenever he expected to win, he invariably won. Whenever he just hoped to win, he almost never won.

I was fascinated by this! I asked him "Mark, what was the difference between when you knew you were going to win and when you just hoped you would win? Those are two very different states!"

His answer startled me. "It was all a function of my level of preparation. Whenever I had done the work to be fully prepared, I knew I was going to win. Whenever I hadn't, I just hoped I would win."

That makes so much sense! Have you ever experienced being so well-prepared for something, be it a test at school, a sales presentation, a competition, or an interview, where you just felt in your cells that you were going to ace it? That's what Mark is talking about. Contrast this with times when you knew you were unprepared, and were just winging it. You were a lot less confident that you would be victorious, weren't you?

Is your preparation at the level that it needs to be in order for you to be able to expect to win?

Most people don't expect to win. They expect to do okay, or get a decent result, and as a result of that type of thinking, that's the best they can ever do.

How can you take your preparation to such a level that you routinely expect to win?

Success Story:

Peter Benes is a web and marketing services entrepreneur. His boyhood dream had been to become a rock and roll singer, but he listened to the authority figures in his life and gave up on that dream to get a "good" job. He did very well, but the dream never died. In the back of his mind, he always wanted to give singing another go.

But he didn't believe in himself, and so he never really took preparing for success very seriously. He would dabble in it, but he never buckled down and did whatever it took to ensure he would be successful. He enrolled in the Finish Line Thinking™ Program, and learned about Principle #3, Expect to Win. He took it on, and made a boyhood dream come true. He joined a band as a singer, and began recording music!

"Nicky's coaching has given me the confidence to pursue goals in areas in which I previously had a lot of self-doubt, namely, my boyhood dream to be a singer/ songwriter. For 6 years, I struggled, thinking I had a bad voice and a bad ear. Nicky showed me that my lack of success was because I was unprepared. My doubts caused me to be lazy in practice. Within 2 months, my preparation went up, and I am well on my way to being a strong and confident performer. I have aggressively been developing myself at a pace that I never have before."

4. Actively surround yourself with the support you need to win

Champions know success is a team sport. They actively recruit the support they need to win. Theresa Dugwell, a 3-time Guinness World Record Holder in ultra-distance running, who runs for 12 hours at a time, had over two dozen people on her success team. She had a fitness coach, a running coach, a nutrition coach, a mindset coach, a masseur, a time-keeper, over a dozen pace runners to run beside her for an hour at a time to keep her going, 2 nutrition sponsors, etc. You might think, did she really need all these people on her team? Her answer is yes, she really did, if she expected to break the Guinness World Record and become a champion.

Have you thought of who you need to surround yourself with to ensure your success at the level of a champion? Who are the people you need to include on your Finish Line Thinking™ championship team?

Success story:

Theresa Dugwell is the founder of Genesis Book Publishing, a company that helps business owners that are not good writers conceive, create, and publish their very own books as a means of branding and differentiating themselves in the marketplace. Full disclosure, the creation of this book has benefitted from her coaching and expertise.

She is also, as mentioned above, a 3-time Guinness World Record Holder, because of this principle.

"I am a big believer in teams. No one can truly succeed on their own. I have run a string of dental clinics, and I have set world records, and my success in both ventures has been predicated on figuring out who I need on my team to help me win, getting them on my team, and then executing. Finish Line Thinking™ is right on the money when it comes to this important principle."

5. Become part of a community of supportive like-minded peers

Birds of a feather flock together. Every mother knows that if she wants her kid to be a good kid, he needs to hang around with good kids. Champions know this principle, and live by it. They hang out with other champions. They motivate, inspire, and learn from each other. They do this consciously. Do you? Are you hanging out with other champions, people like you who are supportive, committed, and like-minded? If you are not, or are unsure, I suggest you re-evaluate your associations and change some or all of them, as necessary.

Mark McKoy's entire career was fueled by hanging out with, learning from, and training with top athletes and champions. Mark used to drive the top Canadian national team track stars to the airport just to be around them and soak up their knowledge and vibe. Donovan Bailey attributes a part of his ongoing success to being part of a community of fellow athletic champions. Top CEOs join business peer groups like eCircle (_www.eCircle.ca_), YPO, TEC, and YEO (Young President's Organization, The Executive Council, and Young Entrepreneur's Organization).

Are there any communities of like-minded Finish Line Thinkers™ out there that you can become a part of? If so, what can you do today to help you join one or more of those communities? If not, how can you create such a community with one or more of your like-minded friends and associates?

Success story:

Michael Palmer has been a successful serial entrepreneur, and his latest company, Pure Bookkeeping North America, teaches bookkeepers how to go from owning their job to having a scalable business. Shortly after we started working together, we went looking for a peer group for Michael. We couldn't find one that fit, so Michael and I teamed up to create one together.

It's called eCircle, Where Entrepreneurs Go To Win™. eCircle is a peer group of supportive, like-minded entrepreneurs that helps ambitious, driven business owners be part of a special environment that will help them grow their business 2 to 10 fold in 12 – 18 months. Being a part of eCircle has helped Michael rapidly grow his business, and to tap into the wisdom of other entrepreneurs in different industries, so that he can move his business forward 10x more rapidly than he has in the past. To check out eCircle, visit _www.eCircle.ca_, and download the free E-book and program curriculum available on that website.

Some members of eCircle, such as OnePlus12 CEO Glenn Estrabillo, have been able to grow their business 12-fold as a result of being part of a community of like-minded peers. Glenn attributes his success in large part to what he got from the fellow members of his peer group.

Michael Palmer says it best! "Finish Line Thinking^{TM} is a brilliant program! Principle #5 has been crucial to my business success, and teaming up with Nicky to create eCircle has helped me move forward toward ever greater business achievement. If you are in business for yourself, I highly recommend being a part of a peer group."

6. Set BIG goals

Champions set BIG goals. They aren't interested or motivated by playing small and setting small goals. They are interested in big goals; huge, massive ones that scare the bejezus out of them, but also excite and inspire them. They don't want to win the local high school race and then rest on their laurels; they want to win the Olympic Final.

Most people play way too small. They set goals that are far below what would stretch them, move them to hustle and grow. They are afraid to set big goals, because they are afraid to fail, and fail spectacularly. So they set goals that are way too easy, way too safe, and ultimately, way too unfulfilling.

They're like Al Bundy on the old 90s TV show "Married with Children", the old high school football star who once scored 4 touchdowns in a single game. That was an awesome accomplishment, but it was also his last serious accomplishment. He peaked at 18 in high school, and he stopped going for it.

What about you? Are you like Mark, or are you like Al? Are your goals BIG, or are they way too small? How can you think bigger than you have ever dared before?

Success Story:

Greg De Koker is the CEO of Evolation, a marketing and branding company. He has had a successful career, but had hit a plateau in the past couple of years. When he joined the Finish Line Thinking™ program, one of the first things I had him do was set his sights much higher. He was afraid at first, but he trusted my coaching and dived right in. Within 6 weeks, he had signed new contracts worth well over six figures to his organization.

"Nicky and the Finish Line Thinking™ program are all about passion, excellence, focus, commitment and accountability. He is a stand for coaching people to live a life they truly love. He continues to make a huge difference in my life and has become a lifelong friend in the process. I'm a better leader, entrepreneur, father and husband – and on target for the best year of my life (including doubling last year's income) – because of Nicky and the Finish Line Thinking™ program. Setting my sights higher led to my best month ever in my business, winning deals worth well over $100,000! With Nicky on your side and in your corner, you will get further faster."

7. Embrace failure, and fail fast

Champions embrace failure. Most people are afraid to fail. They make it mean that they are a failure, so they seek to avoid the experience of failing at all costs. Not champions. Champions embrace failure, fail fast, learn from it, and move on. What about you? Do you embrace failure? Or do you avoid it?

Mark McKoy began his illustrious career at a Toronto-area high school. His dream was to be a sprinter. But his coach said "I already have enough sprinters. I need a hurdler. You can either be the team water boy, or a hurdler. You choose."

Well, Mark chose to be a hurdler. (Sometimes, your path to success won't look the way you think it should. Be ready to take the fork in the road when it offers itself to you.)

The coach said "Great. I have good news and bad news. The good news is you are my hurdler. Congratulations! The bad news is I have no hurdles. Why don't you go on the track, and pretend there are hurdles there every three steps."

Mark saluted like a good soldier, and went on about his business and ran over the imaginary hurdles. Well, that worked fine until the first big track meet, where Mark competed against his fellow hurdlers over a track with actual hurdles on it. The problem was that the hurdles were not placed where Mark's coach had told him they would be, they were actually 10 yards apart. The race was a disaster! Mark hit all the hurdles, and finished dead last.

Most people would give up at this point, disillusioned by their failure. Not Mark, he was going to be good at track no matter what it took. No excuses, choose, and do it now. So he went and found himself some hurdles, and a coach who actually knew what he was doing. The result was that he won OFSAA, the Ontario championship, a few months later.

The lesson? Get a great coach, and don't be afraid to fail, learn, and move on to success.

How can you embrace failure more effectively, fail fast, get the lesson, and move on toward success?

Success Story:

Arnaud Marthouret is a young man I met at a conference, recently finished with school. Initially when we met, he was looking for work. But he set his sights higher, and decided to start a business, even though he had no prior experience as an entrepreneur or even as a salesman. I took him on as a client, and it was immediately apparent that he needed help in generating sales. So I coached him to get on the phone and call people in his target market.

He took it on, in a big way. At first, he met with lots of failure, no one was giving him their time, and he wasn't making any sales. A lot of people would have been tempted to quit, but Arnaud came to each coaching call looking for what he could do differently. We kept tinkering with his phone sales technique, until he started to get appointments. Pretty soon, he became a master at getting appointments, and his business really started to take off.

"Nicky has coached me for the past few months during and after the launch of my new photography business. He was instrumental in taking the business from a good idea to a business with actual sales and revenue. His take-no-prisoners coaching style is not for the faint of heart, but extremely effective in setting goals and -more importantly- putting strategies in place to reach these goals. Nicky cares about people even more than results and I can only highly recommend him to anyone willing to become the highest performing, best possible version of themselves."

8. Get the best coach, not just a great coach

In 1990, Mark was approached by his good friend Colin Jackson of the UK, who was the #1 hurdler in the world at that time. Colin asked Mark to come to the UK and train with him and his coach, Malcolm Arnold, who was the best hurdles coach in the world.

Mark jumped at the chance. He moved to the UK, and began training with Colin and Malcolm.

On his first day at the track, Malcolm said "Go run over the hurdles one time for me."

Mark went out and did as he was told. It took him all of 13 seconds to do that. Malcolm noticed something that no one else who had ever worked with Mark had noticed before. He noticed that Mark's left foot was slightly crooked whenever he landed on it, such that he lost about an inch versus if his foot had landed straight.

He told Mark what he noticed. Initially, Mark was unimpressed. He said to Malcolm "I came all this way for an inch?"

Malcolm said "Ah, but it's not just an inch. You take 39 strides with your left leg in a race. It's actually 39 inches."

That changed everything. 39 inches in an Olympic race like the 110 meter hurdles was often the difference between first place and 4th place, between a Gold Medal, and no medal.

He told Mark "Concentrate, and your foot will go straight."

So Mark did what he was told. He ran over the hurdles one or two more times, concentrating on his foot going straight, and the problem was solved. Two years later, at the Barcelona Olympics, during the 110 meter high hurdles finals, Mark got off to his patented bullet start, and went on to win the Olympic Gold Medal.

His winning margin?

39 inches!!!

This is a powerful principle. For 13 years, Mark had been one of the top hurdlers in the world! He had worked with some great coaches, and had some great training partners. But no one, not his coaches, not his training partners, not even he himself, had caught this mistake, for 13 years! And he was a very accomplished athlete, winning national and international championships, and setting 2 world records during that time period. But he never won the big races, such as the Olympics or the World Championships.

In his very first training session with the best coach in the world, he got the coaching that made the difference that made him the Olympic Champion, and the oldest person ever to win his event. And it took all of 13 seconds for that coach to make that difference.

13 years of frustration versus 13 seconds of gold medal coaching.

The questions you want to ask yourself are: do you have the best possible coaching in the areas that are important to you? If you do, great! If you don't, how can you find out who the very best coaches are, and go and engage with them? It can save you years of frustration!

Maybe you're in a situation where you're not sure who the best coaches are. The question to ask yourself in this situation is, how can I keep increasing the quality of coaches and coaching that I'm getting?

Success story:

Micah Munro is a top performing real estate agent with ReMax in Toronto. His rise to the top of the ranks in the past few years has been meteoric, where he doubled his gross commission income from $250,000 to $500,000 in just one year. His goal for the next year was to increase it again, to $800,000. But the year didn't start off so great, and he began to doubt himself. Doubt is deadly, for doubt kills the warrior!

He decided to join the Finish Line Thinking™ program. I quickly saw that his doubts were preventing him from taking committed action. I created a series of daily rituals for him to follow to get into a peak state, and I had him commit to daily prospecting. He took it on like a true champion. Within 2 months, his doubts melted away, and the results on the board had him on track to not just $800,000, but over $1 million!

"I am a big believer in coaching, and I have and continue to work with some great coaches. They have been a big part of my success to date. But working with Nicky and the Finish Line Thinking™ program brought something to me that none of my other coaches have done, and that's a rock solid focus on having the mindset of a champion performer. The work we have done together has made a massive difference for me, in a short period of time. Nicky says that doubt kills the warrior, or the warrior kills the doubt! I have killed the doubt!"

9. Develop the Heart of a Champion

Champions have the biggest hearts. A true champion is generous and giving of himself, his time, his knowledge, and his support. There is a lie that's out there, that anyone who is successful, who ever made something of himself, did it by stabbing someone else in the back, stepping on people, or stealing from them. While it's true that some people get ahead this way, a true champion never does.

Let me illustrate this with a powerful story from my friend Mark McKoy.

When he was 18, he met the then holder of the 110 meter hurdles world record, Renaldo Nehemiah. They were both running at a track meet being held at Maple Leaf Gardens. In the finals, Renaldo came first, and Mark came last. After the race, Mark plucked up his courage and went up to Renaldo and asked him for his advice on what he should do to get better. To Mark's astonishment, Renaldo sat down with him for an hour and gave him a complete plan to take him to the next level. Mark followed his advice, and it paid off: he got himself a scholarship to a university in the US.

That taught him – and me -- something. He used to think successful people didn't have the interest or the time to help others. He thought that they would want to keep their secrets to themselves so that they could stay ahead of the competition. Renaldo showed Mark just how wrong he was. Since then, Mark and I have learned that most successful people want to give back and to contribute to others. Sometimes this fulfills them more than anything else they do.

A true champion has a heart of gold, he uplifts those around him by the power of his example, and by sharing his knowledge. That's the mark of real greatness.

Where and how can you be more generous, especially to someone who is seeking a mentor? How can you give more than you are currently giving?

Success Story:

Max Carbone is the founder and Principal Consultant at Team Works, *www.teamworksweb.com*, a consultancy that specializes in strategic planning and performance optimization for companies such as Royal

LePage, Air Canada Pilots Association, PwC Consulting, and other Fortune 100 organizations. Max has a pretty unique problem, he has so much business, he can't handle it all by himself! He joined the Finish Line Thinking™ program, and really took this principle to heart. He has set the stage for increasing the size of his business, and taking more time off, by bringing in people to help him deliver on the projects he has taken on with his clients.

In his industry, it's a rarity for owners to bring in their potential competitors to do work with and get cozy with their customers. But Max didn't see it that way, he saw it as an opportunity to help some colleagues grow and expand their capacities and their businesses, and as a result, he is now in a position to double his time off and his income!

"Nicky and the Finish Line Thinking™ program have been truly great for me and Team Works. I am by nature a generous person, and it's wonderful to have a hardnosed business coaching program validate generosity as a key success tool."

21

10. You're either addicted or committed. Commit

You are either run by your addictions or by your commitments. What do I mean by that? Here are a couple of examples:

You may say you have a commitment to get up at 6 AM every day and workout. But when the alarm rings, you hit the snooze button repeatedly, and don't get up until 6:45 AM. This leaves you no time to workout. Here, you are addicted to sleep, and that addiction won out over your commitment to workout.

You may say that you are committed to eating healthy as a way of life. But when you go to your friend's party and they offer you double-layered chocolate cake made with extra sugar, you have 3 pieces! Here, you are addicted to cake, and that addiction defeated your commitment to eat healthy.

You may say you are committed to doubling your sales this year. But instead of making prospecting calls two hours a day, you go surf the web or clean up your desk. Your addiction to distracting yourself is defeating your commitment to increasing your sales.

Champions are committed. They don't sleep in. They don't eat chocolate cake. They don't go out drinking Friday night. They go to bed early, they wake up early, they eat right, and they cut out the alcohol, because they are committed to winning, and not addicted to sleeping, eating cake, or boozing it up on a Friday night. They don't distract themselves by surfing the web or straightening out their desk. They make prospecting calls, day in and day out, they make sales appointments, and they close sales, because they are committed to winning, not to distracting themselves with trivia.

Are you run by your commitments or by your addictions? If you're honest with yourself, you realize that like all of us, you have some commitments and some addictions.

Ask yourself this question: in what areas can I move out of being addicted and into being committed?

For example, I have a commitment to be the leanest I have ever been. I have an addiction to snacking on organic rice crackers before going to bed. This is an area where I am going to move out of my addiction and into my commitment!

Success Story:

I am not only the Founder and Head Thinking Coach of the Finish Line Thinking™ program, I am also a client.

One of my addictions prior to learning this principle had been to distract myself by surfing the internet instead of making prospecting calls. If you are in sales, and I submit you, like all of us, are; then you can relate to this. Almost anything appears to be more fun than making cold calls!

My addiction to distracting myself was winning over my commitment to make prospecting calls. I took this principle on, and began living more from commitment than addiction. I made lots of prospecting calls in the latter half of last year. The result was fantastic! I doubled my revenues in the second half of the year over the first half, and year over year, I recorded a 55% increase in business revenues.

"To quote Sy Sperling of the Hair Club for Men, I am not only the President of the Finish Line Thinking™ program, I am also a client. And a very satisfied one at that!"

11. Seek to be held accountable

Champions seek to be held accountable. They know that without accountability, they will falter and fail. As such, they seek to be held accountable by their Community of Champions. What's the Community of Champions? It's a special community composed of champions, who meet, network, and hold one another accountable. I'll say more about this later.

Accountability is very important for a champion. Mark was held accountable by his Community of Champions, which included his best friend and training partner Colin Jackson, who was then the best hurdler in the world, and his coach, Malcolm Arnold, who was the best hurdles coach in the world. Their very presence in his Community of Champions held his feet to the fire and ensured that he trained hard for the 1992 Olympics. All this training paid off, because he won the Olympic Gold Medal at these Olympics.

Are you being held accountable, by someone other than yourself, someone who won't let you off the hook? If you are, congratulations; if not, who can hold you accountable? How can you have yourself be held accountable at a higher level, so that you stay on track with your mission critical tasks?

The eCircle is one such Community of Champions, created specifically for entrepreneurs. If you are an entrepreneur, or a professional salesperson such as a real estate broker, insurance broker, or stock broker, and are not currently part of a Community of Champions, check out eCircle at _www.eCircle.ca_.

Success Story:

Glenn Estrabillo is a real estate investor, who was successful enough at real estate investing that he was able to retire at age 28! But he was too young, too energetic and too purpose-driven to stay retired. He got back in the game, and joined an early version of the eCircle Community of Champions that I ran. Within 6 months, he got an unexpected piece of feedback from the Circle that helped him increase his income and his net worth 12-fold!

"When I joined the [eCircle] that Nicky ran, I was primarily investing in single family homes. I had never bought anything larger than a duplex. One of the members of the [eCircle] suggested that I expand my horizons, and buy an apartment building. He said that the hard part was knowing how to get investors to invest in me and my vision, and since I obviously knew how to do that, I needed to think bigger and get them to invest in a bigger vision. It had never occurred to me to do that before! I took his advice, and to my amazement, my investors bought into my bigger vision, and I bought my first 12-unit apartment building a few months later! That increased my income and net worth 12-fold in no time at all. The concept of being a part of a Community of Champions really works!"

12. Embrace Mastery

W e live in a society that worships the new: the latest fashions, the latest movies, the latest diet, and yes, the latest fitness craze. But are trends really the answer?

No and hell, no!

If you follow trends, you'll never be a champion. Period.

All champions seek mastery in their field. Mastery lives in doing the same things over and over and over again, until they become encoded in your DNA, until they are transparent to you.

The top performers in any field will tell you that; be it a master saleswoman, an award-winning actor, or a renowned heart surgeon.

Here's how Mark put it to me; "What I noticed was that all the Gold Medal-winning athletes and their coaches did and counseled the same fundamental exercise routines to get into peak condition so that they could compete and win. They weren't necessarily better athletes than second and third place finishers, in many cases the people they beat had more natural ability than they did. But in almost every instance, they were in worse shape, because they did not follow the routines of the champions."

The routines of champions! What a brilliant and elegant phrase! Champions are willing to do the hard work necessary to become masters at what they do. John Wooden, the legendary coach of the UCLA Bruins basketball team, was famous for insisting on mastery from his players. He would take kids who were the best players in the country, and tell them to do a jump shot 500 times, then a lay-up 500 times, and so on. This had his players be ready to take that shot when the game was on the line with a confidence born of preparation and mastery. That's how he won 7 straight national championships (10 in 12 years), a feat no other team or coach in any sport has come close to equaling.

Are you embracing mastery in the areas of your most important priorities? How can you up your level of mastery? What would it take?

Success Story:

Victor Menasce, the author of The Great Canadian Takeover, is a Canadian real estate investor who primarily purchases US real estate. Victor has had a lot of success in raising money to purchase American-based property, and he has a real knack for finding under-valued deals. His key impediment was that he was spending a lot of time on other things, such as administrative issues and even non-core business activities, such as mentoring and coaching other real estate investors.

Shortly after he signed on to the Finish Line Thinking™ program, he got the importance of this principle. He hired an assistant to take on his admin duties, cut back on non-core activities like coaching, and began a monomaniacal focus on the things he did best, which happened to be the most fundamentally important parts of successful real estate investing on a large scale, finding great deals and raising money for investment.

"Embracing Mastery is an important principle for me, because it has me focus on what really drives my success forward, and not on issues that are distractions or could easily be handled by someone else. I'm able to grow my business bigger and faster by taking this principle on."

13. Take on Daily Disciplines

This is the most important principle. Ask any champion, and he (or she) will tell you, that what makes him (or her) a champion is that he (or she) is willing to do what others are not willing to do. My fitness mentor, Olympic Champion Mark McKoy, shared this insight with me. He told me that on his way to the Gold Medal, he came across many people that were more talented and more physically gifted than he was.

In fact, he was kind of short for a hurdler. He was only 5' 11", and most hurdlers are at least 6' 2". But Mark was willing to do what was needed to win, and some of his more talented competitors were not. Mark spent 8 hours a day, 7 days a week, 50 weeks a year training to win the Olympic Gold. He ate right, and he got the rest he needed to recuperate. When his buddies wanted to go out drinking on a Saturday night, he stayed home and went to bed early, so he could get up at 5 AM and go to the track and train. That kind of daily dedication took a (relatively) short, skinny kid from Canada all the way to qualifying for 5 Olympics, and winning the Gold Medal.

My former business partner, Olympic Champion Donovan Bailey, taught me the importance of daily visualization. Every day, he would visualize himself running, and winning the Olympic final, hundreds of times a day. This daily practice had a dual purpose. First, it would help him relax and de-stress, because he was in an alpha-theta brain wave state, which is akin to meditation or prayer. Second, he was engaging in Finish Line Thinking™, by clearly visualizing victory, he built his inner belief in his ultimate goal, heightening his expectations and powering him to victory.

To double or even triple your current success rate, and cross that Finish Line as a champion, you need to take on daily disciplines that you stick to, just like a champion. Take on Daily Disciplines! Daily Disciplines Are What Champions Do! The 5 Most Important Daily Disciplines are:

1. Daily Exercise & Healthy Eating
2. Daily Success Rituals
3. Daily De-stressing
4. Daily Accountability
5. Daily Commitments

Bonus!

6. Daily Finish Line Thinking™

1. Daily Exercise & Healthy Eating

Daily exercise is a no-brainer for all champions. Champions know that to become and remain a champion, they must take care of their bodies, and ensure that they are in peak condition. This is critical to their success. Daily exercise is a key discipline that helps them ensure their success. Are you willing to embrace this daily discipline?

What are some ways that you can make sure you exercise every day? You don't have to go to a gym every day, or even commit to an hour every day. What if you did at least 10 pushups, 10 sit-ups, and 10 squats, every day? What if you had some of your business meetings be walking meetings, where you took a colleague out for a walk, talked over an important issue, and got in 30 minutes of exercise?

The point is that if you make the commitment, and you follow through, you will increase your mental and physical strength, just like a champion.

Daily healthy eating is even more important than daily exercise. 80% of your success in keeping your body in a peak state of health depends on what you eat. Champions know this, which is why they are committed to a discipline of daily healthy eating. Are you willing to embrace this daily discipline?

What are some ways in which you can do this?

2. Daily Success Rituals

Daily success rituals are a key part of any champion's arsenal of success. Every champion I know has daily success rituals that they follow. Success rituals are powerful because they help you raise your energy, and pull success toward you. They are like powerful magnets, and the success you seek is like a piece of steel caught in their orbit. Here are 3 that I use myself, and teach my clients to their massive benefit:

The Finish Line Thinking™ Results Ritual

I got the idea for creating this particular ritual from Tony Robbins. He taught me that success was all about being in a Peak State, and if you are not in a peak state, it's easy to get into one.

This is especially important for you if you are a performance-driven individual. Have you started a day or gone into an important sales presentation or business meeting feeling less than your best? What was it like for you? What was the result?

Chances are, it was something less than what you wanted.

To achieve Peak Results, you need to be in Peak State!

Why?

Because Peak States cause Peak Performance!

To get into a Peak State at the start your day, or to prepare for an important meeting, do the Finish Line Thinking™ Results Ritual. It takes just 5 minutes, and can make the difference between a Peak Result and No Result!

Here's how it works:

3 Simple Steps

Step 1: Listen to music that stirs your soul

Research shows that music you love has powerful effects on your body and your state, by releasing adrenaline and dopamine into your body, and by making you feel energized and happy at the same time. What piece of music stirs your soul? Put it on your playlist and have it handy!

Step 2: Move your body

Emotion is caused by motion! Move your body! Clap your hands together, pump your fists, jump up and down, and say "Yes" 10 times! Create your very own power move, one that changes your state. Create a loud one and a quiet one, for when you're in public spaces.

Step 3: Ask Intelligent Questions

The quality of your life depends on the quality of questions you ask yourself. The human mind is amazing, it will answer any question you put before it. If you ask it negative, disempowering questions, the answers will lower your energy. If you ask it intelligent, empowering questions, it will put you into a peak state! Here are the 5 Intelligent Questions all Finish Line Thinkers™ ask:

1. What am I happy about, today?
2. What am I excited about, today?
3. Who can I make a difference for, today?

4. How can I attract my ideal clients, today?
5. How can I give my best, today?

Bonus Question:

6. I wonder who's the lucky Son of a Gun that gets to meet me, today?

The Finish Line Thinking™ Gratitude Ritual

If you are like most people, you don't spend a lot of time in gratitude. You probably spend a lot more time complaining than you do being grateful for what you have in your life. How do I know this? Because for much of my life, I was like this! And if you look at the world around you, you will see that complaining and negativity are the way of the world.

90% of news stories are negative, which are essentially a complaint. Most people you encounter "trauma share", or talk about what is, has gone, is going, and will likely be going wrong with them, their spouse, their kids, the world, etc. You get the picture, right?

The problem with this is that listening to complaints and bad news, or even worse, spreading complaints and bad news, lowers your energy, which means you are no longer in a Peak State, and you will no longer be able to achieve Peak Results.

The Finish Line Thinking™ Gratitude Ritual is a powerful way to neutralize all this negativity and raise your energy. And it's simple and easy to do. Just think about something or someone in your life that you are grateful for, and why. Feel the feelings of gratitude in your body. This step is crucial! Don't simply recite or read off a list! Really take your time, and linger on each person or thing, until the feelings of gratitude are strongly present in your body.

For example, I'm really grateful for my father. He is a great man. He taught me by example what it is to be generous, kind, and strong. He was a great provider for his family, and he gave away much of what he made to other people. He also made a bunch of mistakes in his life, and I learned from watching those, too. I am the man I am in large part because of my father. I am grateful to have been his son.

I am also really grateful for where I live! I own a great condo that's a one minute walk from the beach. One whole minute! In the summertime, sometimes I take the afternoon off, grab my beach towel and a good book, and go catch some rays! I am very grateful for this!

31

Here are some questions to get you going:

- Who do you love? Who loves you?
- What is the wealth you have currently in your life? Technology? Choices? Family? Friends? Books? Music? Ideas? Opportunities?
- What's right in your life? What's the best it's ever been?
- What's beautiful? Magical? Special?

Get the idea? Good! Now do this every day for 10 minutes, and you will soon be vibrating with massively enhanced energy and power, and attract success to you more easily and quickly.

The Finish Line Thinking™ Incantation Ritual

I learned this from a buddy of mine who is a former Navy SEAL. The Navy SEALs are probably the toughest warriors on earth. Just getting into the SEALs makes you a champion of the first rank.

An incantation is a powerful, positive phrase that you repeat to yourself over and over again, loud and proud, while moving your body. Doing it to rhythm and music will make it even more powerful!

As you jump, run, or walk, use the music, use your body, and use your mind to reinforce your incantations.

Move with a sense of power and excitement and link it to a sense of certainty as you boom out your incantations over and over again!

Here is a powerful one I use with my clients that you might like:

I will make me a champion!
I will WIN, not lose!
I will SOAR, not fall!
I will PERSIST, not falter!
I will SUCCEED, not fail!
LEAP UP! LEAP UP! LEAP UP!
YES! YES! YES, YES, YES, YES!

Speak what you INTEND to become. Speak with power, certainty and intensity.

Do this for 10 minutes a day.

3. Daily De-stressing

Champions are under an enormous amount of stress. The level of focus and concentration required to prepare for and win Olympic Gold or set a world record is enormous, and without a daily practice to dissipate this stress, they would never be able to become – let alone remain -- a champion. Are you willing to embrace this daily discipline?

Meditation, prayer, going for a walk with someone you love, playing with your children, etc., are a few examples of daily de-stressing activities you can commit to.

4. Daily Accountability

Champions know that without someone to be accountable to, they could easily backslide and avoid doing some of the hard but necessary activities that allow them to win and be champions. Let's face it, not all things you have to do in order to become a champion are fun! Champions know that, and to make sure they are never tempted to take shortcuts, they have accountability structures in place, like coaches, training buddies, etc. Just by being there, a coach will keep you on your toes and on track in getting things done! Are you willing to embrace this daily discipline?

5. Daily Commitments

Champions make daily commitments in areas that are out of their comfort zone, but are necessary to moving their success forward. John Wooden, the legendary UCLA Bruins basketball coach, taught his players to take 500 layups in a row, until they were able to do it automatically, without thinking about it, with the game on the line. That's why his teams won 7 straight national championships! My friend Leslie Benczik, a champion realtor with ReMax, makes prospecting cold calls 3 hours a day. This discipline took him from being a rookie sales rep to Top 20 in Canada, earning a fabulous income in the process. He was willing to do something way out of his comfort zone as a daily discipline, and it led him to success. What is a daily discipline out of your comfort zone that you know would take you to greater success?

Bonus! 6. Daily Finish Line Thinking™

So what the heck is Daily Finish Line Thinking™?

Simple.

It's keeping the finish line in mind, every day. Champions know what their finish line is. Do you know what yours looks like? Are you focused on it? If you are, awesome! If you are not, you'll never be a champion! What's your finish line?

Mark McKoy's finish line was the Olympic Gold Medal. So was Donovan Bailey's. Theresa Dugwell's was to break a Guinness World Record. Darren Lenkorn's was to be North American Karate Champion. These are all champions that I know and have studied in order to understand how champions think and win.

If you want to be a champion every day, you have got to be thinking about your finish line every day, about how you're going to cross it, with your arms in the air, yelling "Yes! I've done it!"

When I was studying with Donovan Bailey, who is a 5-time Olympic and World Champion in the 100 m and 4 x 100 m relay races, he told me that his expectation of victory was so high that he actually visualized himself winning the big race 150,000 times! That's right, 150,000 times! His expectation was built to a fever pitch through powerful visualization techniques.

The Finish Line Thinking™ Visioning Process

Next, we will go through a Finish Line Thinking™ Visioning Process, to help you get crystal clear on what your finish line looks like, and to create a plan to get you there.

To get from where you are to the Finish Line involves going through a process. The first step is to help you understand how you currently think, versus how a champion thinks. To this end, we have designed the Finish Line Thinking™ Scorecard. It's a quick and simple way for you to see what your current thinking is like. The scorecard is below. Take a moment to fill it out and add up your score.

The Finish Line Thinking Scorecard™

To help you clearly understand your current situation, try The Finish Line Thinking Scorecard™. Rate your reactions to each pair of phrases. Decide where you lie on the scale from 1 to 10. Add up your total from each column. Speak to one of our advisors to understand the significance of your score.

	1	2	3	4	5	6	7	8	9	10	
I do not have clear goals	1	2	3	4	5	6	7	8	9	10	I have clear, well-defined goals
My thoughts & attitudes often sabotage my success	1	2	3	4	5	6	7	8	9	10	My thoughts & attitudes power my success forward
I am frustrated that I have not achieved what I am capable of	1	2	3	4	5	6	7	8	9	10	I am grateful that I have achieved what I am capable of
I do not really believe that I can achieve success as I define it	1	2	3	4	5	6	7	8	9	10	I really believe that I can achieve success as I define it
I am not aware of the deep programming that might be negatively affecting my performance	1	2	3	4	5	6	7	8	9	10	I have reprogrammed my thinking to achieve top performance
I am unfit and out of shape	1	2	3	4	5	6	7	8	9	10	I am very fit and energized
I am not good at asking for support when I need it	1	2	3	4	5	6	7	8	9	10	I ask for and have support when I need it
I am not clear about how to achieve my goals	1	2	3	4	5	6	7	8	9	10	I am clear about how to achieve my goals
I am not having any fun	1	2	3	4	5	6	7	8	9	10	I am having a blast
I do not feel I am achieving my full potential	1	2	3	4	5	6	7	8	9	10	I feel I am achieving my full potential
ADD COLUMN TOTALS											YOUR SCORE _____

If you scored below an 80, at least in some respects, you are not employing Finish Line Thinking™. You could benefit from learning and applying the concepts of the program to your life and your most important priorities.

Here are two important questions for you to answer. Write your answers out in the space below:

Question 1: Why did you give yourself that score?

Questions 2: What do you think you need to do to improve your score?

If you have answered these questions thoroughly and honestly, congratulations! You have taken an important step toward re-aligning your thinking, and becoming a Finish Line Thinker™!

The next question is very important. Why? Because it will help you get started with defining your vision of what your Finish Line looks like.

As we said earlier, to get from where you are to the Finish Line involves going through a process. The next step is to create a vision of the Finish Line for you. If you were at the Finish Line, and feeling like a champion, what would you have already accomplished? Take 5 minutes to visualize & write down what it looks like for you to be at the finish line as a champion, in all the areas of your life that are important to you.

Describe in detail.

Here are some examples to help get your thinking started:

- 29 inch waist, 8-pack abs, ripped and shredded body (man)
- Size 6, trim and tight thighs, butt, and tummy (woman)
- 175 pounds, 10% body fat (man)
- 135 pounds, 20% body fat (woman)
- Obtain 50 seller listings this year
- Sell 60 homes this year
- Add $10 million in assets under management to my book of business
- Hire a buyer agent
- Hire an assistant
- Grow company revenues 50% a year for the next 5 years
- Sell my company for $100 million in 5 years
- Triple the size of my database
- Grow my business to help 5000 clients
- Write a book, and use it to brand myself and market my business
- Vacation 2 months per year
- Daily 1 hour workout
- Daily ½ hour meditation/de-stress
- Speaking 50x per year, making $10,000 per speech
- Own $10 million in income producing real estate
- Read 25 new books a year
- Give up indulging anger
- Set a big fitness goal
- Break a world record

Top 3 are:

1. 175 pounds, 10% body fat (man), 135 pounds, 20% body fat (woman)
2. Grow my business 50% a year for the next 5 years
3. Vacation 2 months a year

Now it's time for you to jot down a few of yours:

Vision Question

If you were at the finish line [1], and feeling like a champion, what would you have accomplished?

1.

2.

3.

4.

5.

6.

7.

8.

9.

10.

Circle your top 3.

Now it's gut check time: How committed are you to working on these, on a scale of 1 to 10? Be honest! Don't write 10 if you're not a 10! Write it down:

1.

2.

3.

The final question is all about helping you connect your vision of the Finish Line to your emotions. We all like to think our intellect runs the show, but the truth is, your emotions are the primary drivers of your behavior, and if you want to get to the Finish Line as a Champion, you have to connect your goals to your expected positive feelings!

---

[1]By finish line, I mean the finish line of your most important priorities, not the end of your life! You still have many more races to run!

If you were at the finish line, what feelings would you experience?

1.

2.

3.

4.

5.

6.

7.

The next step is for us to begin to make a plan on how you will accomplish these goals.

Write down the top 10 things you think you need to do in order to make these things happen. Here are a few examples:

1. Daily Eating Plan – create it and stick to it
2. Daily Workout Plan
3. Create a Plan to find 1,000 new leads for my database
4. Create a Daily Prospecting Plan to get listing/sales appointments
5. Get on radio, internet, and TV about my book, to generate new leads
6. Test drive the plan with one-one-one appointments
7. Book 20 minutes of reading time per day
8. Set up referral arrangements with referral sources

Now jot down yours:

1.

2.

3.

4.

5.

6.

7.

8.

9.

10.

Next, create a detailed, step-by-step plan to help you get there, using Finish Line Thinking™ concepts and processes. Then you are off and to the races, and to the Finish Line, a Champion!

The End

GET HELP WITH WINNING AT YOUR FINISH LINE

If you would like help with winning at your Finish Line, we offer a free Starter Session called The Finish Line Thinking™ Visioning Process. During the session you will:

- Clarify what your Finish Line looks like.
- Identify the exact steps you need to take to ensure your victory on your top priority
- Create a plan of action for you to follow, detailed and exact like a Champion's
- Determine which of the 13 Principles will make the biggest difference for you right now, and apply them immediately
- Infuse you with the self-confidence of a champion
- Prepare you for victory
- The 90 minute Finish Line Thinking™ Visioning Process is provided free of charge to qualified candidates. To book your session, call 416 629 7481, or email *info@finishlinethinking.com*.

Nicky Billou is an author, speaker, businessman, coach, and father of two boys living in Toronto. He has worked with some of the world's most celebrated champions, including Olympic Gold Medalists Mark McKoy and Donovan Bailey, as well as ultra-distance Guinness World Record Holder Theresa Dugwell, and champions in business and personal development; including top CEOs, entrepreneurs, and real estate agents.

HIRE NICKY BILLOU TO SPEAK AT YOUR
NEXT CORPORATE EVENT!

"I have seen the best speakers in the world, and Nicky outshines them all. He is a Gold Medal level speaker."

Olympic Gold medalist and keynote speaker Mark McKoy, Barcelona 1992, 110 m hurdles

Hire Nicky to come speak at your next corporate function or event!

What does it take to be a top performer? Join the numerous companies who have already been inspired by Nicky's compelling personal story, and his exceptional knowledge of high performance, leadership, success and wellness.

Let Nicky tailor a talk that meets the exclusive needs of your audience. For more information, or to book Nicky to speak at your next function, contact him on Twitter *@NickyBillou*, or via email at *info@ finishlinethinking.com*.